for 1000+ tutorials ... use our
free site .... drawinghowtodraw.com

Copyright © Rachel A. Goldstein, DrawingHowToDraw.com, 2016

All rights reserved. No part of this book may be reproduced or transmitted in any form or by any means whatsoever without express written permission from the author, except in the case of brief quotations embodied in critical articles and reviews. Please refer all pertinent questions to the publisher. All rights reserved. No part of this book may be reproduced or transmitted in any form or by any means, electronic or mechanical, including photocopying, recording, or by an information storage and retrieval system - except by a reviewer who may quote brief passages in a review to be printed in a magazine or newspaper - without permission in writing from the publisher.

BY RACHEL GOLDSTEIN

HOW TO DRAW KAWAII CUTE ANIMALS + CHARACTERS 2

EASY TO DRAW ANIME AND MANGA DRAWING FOR KIDS

CARTOONING FOR KIDS + LEARNING HOW TO DRAW SUPER CUTE KAWAII ANIMALS, CHARACTERS, DOODLES & THINGS

REMEMBER... NOBODY GETS IT PERFECT THE FIRST TIME
PRACTICE MAKES PERFECT!
ALL ARTISTS WERE ONCE KIDS...JUST LIKE U!

VISIT
DRAWINGHOWTODRAW.COM
FOR HUNDREDS
OF FREE
TUTORIALS
FOR KIDS
LIKE YOU!

KISSING KITTIES

1.

2.

3. Letter "V" ears
   Erase on dotted line

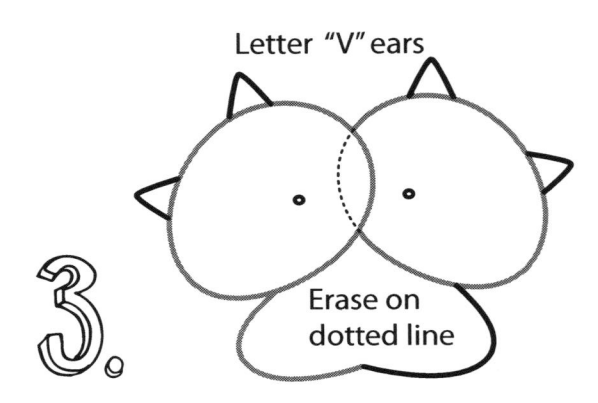

4. Don't draw the dotted line
   "?" shaped tails

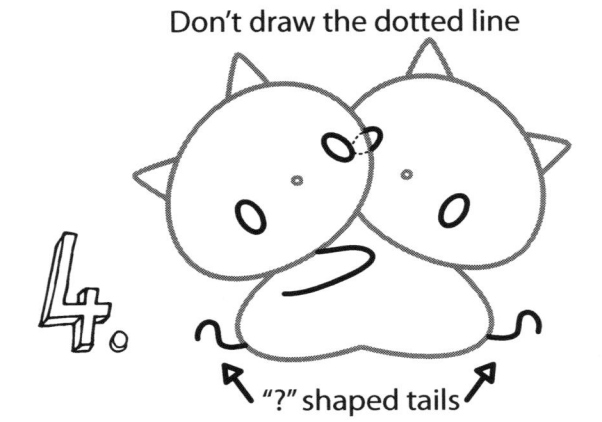

5. Letter "V" shape
   #2 shape

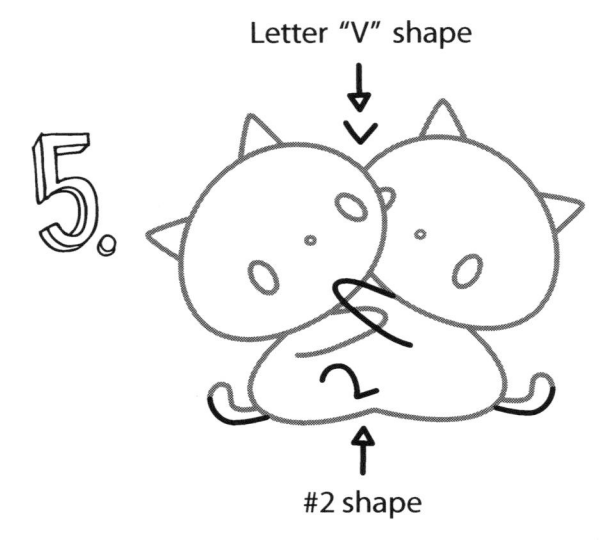

6.

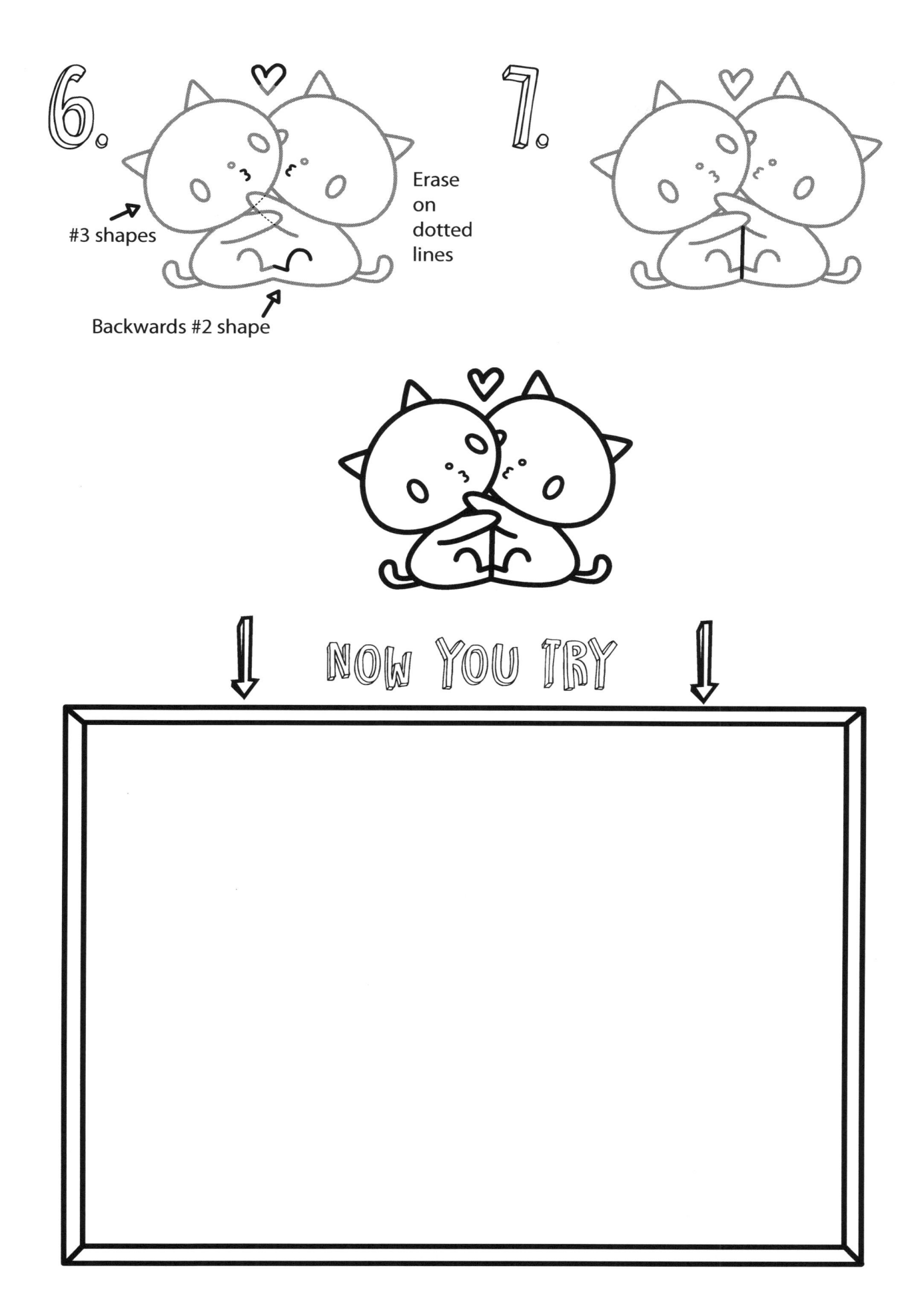

← #3 shapes

Erase on dotted lines

↑ Backwards #2 shape

7.

NOW YOU TRY

LLAMA UNICORN

1. Draw cloud shapes. Don't draw the dotted lines.

2.

3. Draw letter "U" shapes

4. Draw letter "m" and "v" shapes

5. Draw letter "Y" shape

6.

Erase on dotted lines

NOW YOU TRY

SPUNKY CACTUS

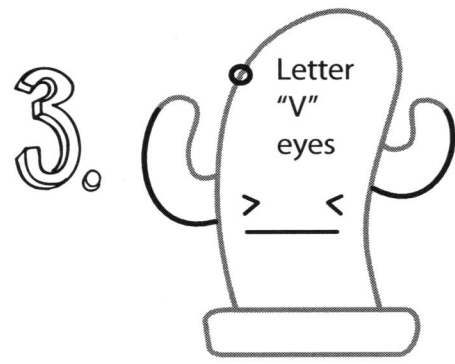

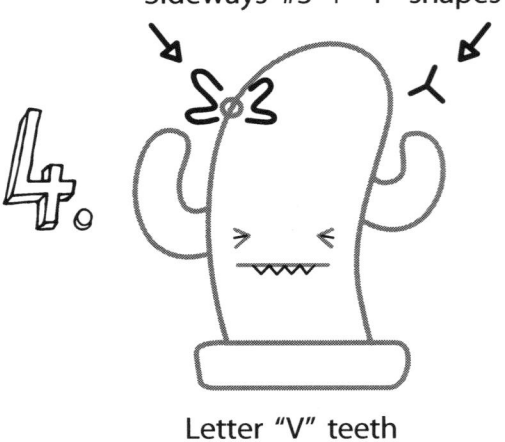

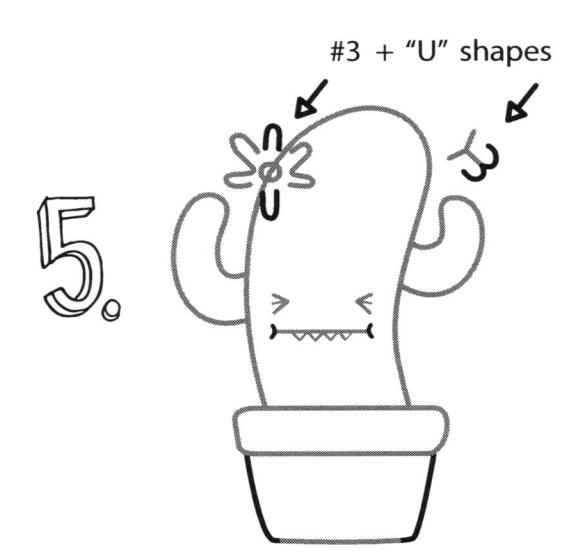

1.

2. Letter "S" shapes

3. Letter "V" eyes

4. Sideways #3 + "Y" shapes

Letter "V" teeth

5. #3 + "U" shapes

6.

1.

Erase on dotted line

NOW YOU TRY

GIDDY CHIPMUNK

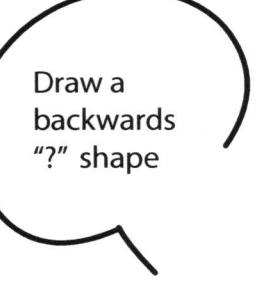

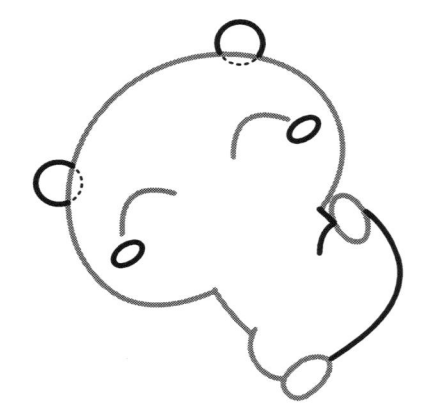

1. Draw a backwards "?" shape

2.

3. Don't draw the dotted lines

4. Draw letter "U" arms

5. Letter "W" shape

⬇ NOW YOU TRY ⬇

KID IN DRAGON COSTUME

1. Upside down letter "U" shape

2.

3. #3 shape

"V" + "U" shapes

4. Letter "U" shapes

"Y" shape

5.

6.

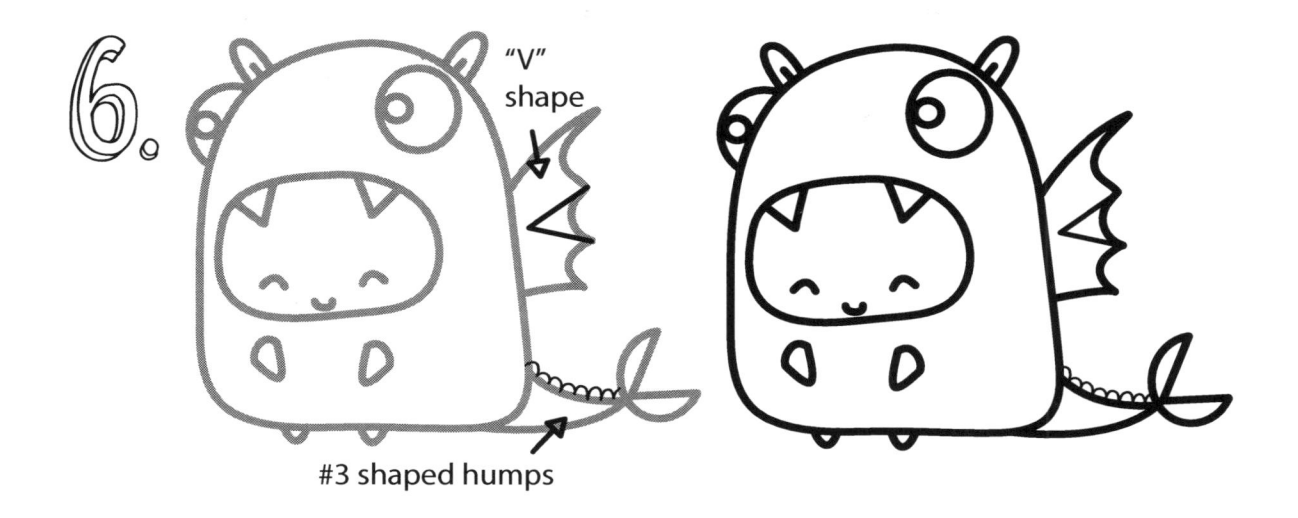

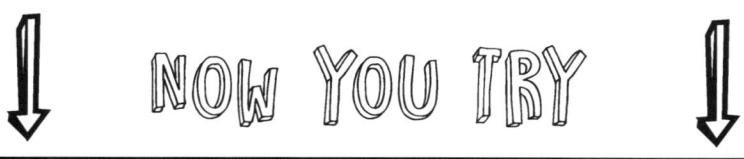

"V" shape

#3 shaped humps

⬇ NOW YOU TRY ⬇

BEAR AND HIS BOY

1.

2.

Letter "w" shape

3.

Letters "M" + "C" shapes

4.

Letters "c" + "w" shapes

5.

#3 shaped hands

Erase on dotted line

6.

"Y" + "J" + "C" shapes

7.

Erase on dotted lines

NOW YOU TRY

CAT AND HER KITTEN

1.  Draw letters "L" + "M"

2.

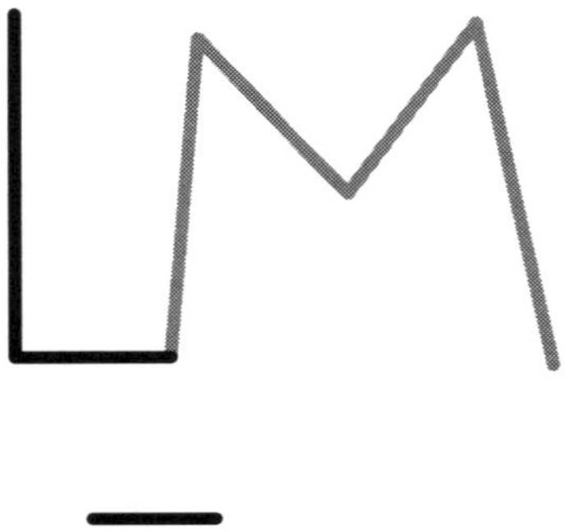

3.

4. 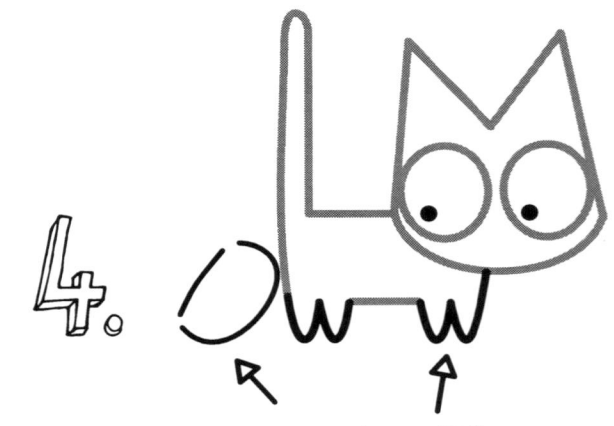 Draw a letter "D" + sideways #3 shapes

5.

6.

7.

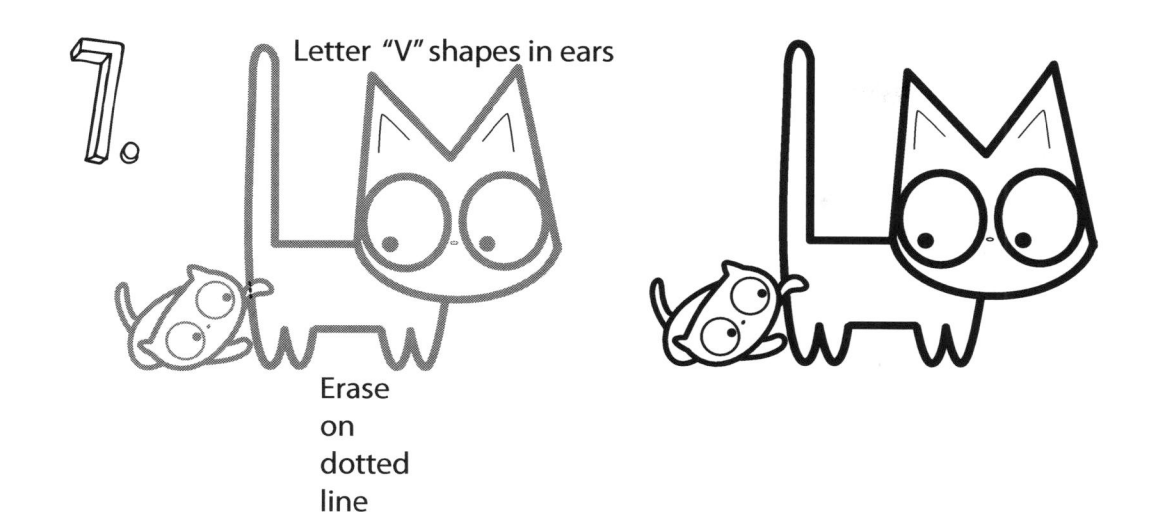

Letter "V" shapes in ears

Erase on dotted line

NOW YOU TRY

FOX AND THE CUTE BALLOON

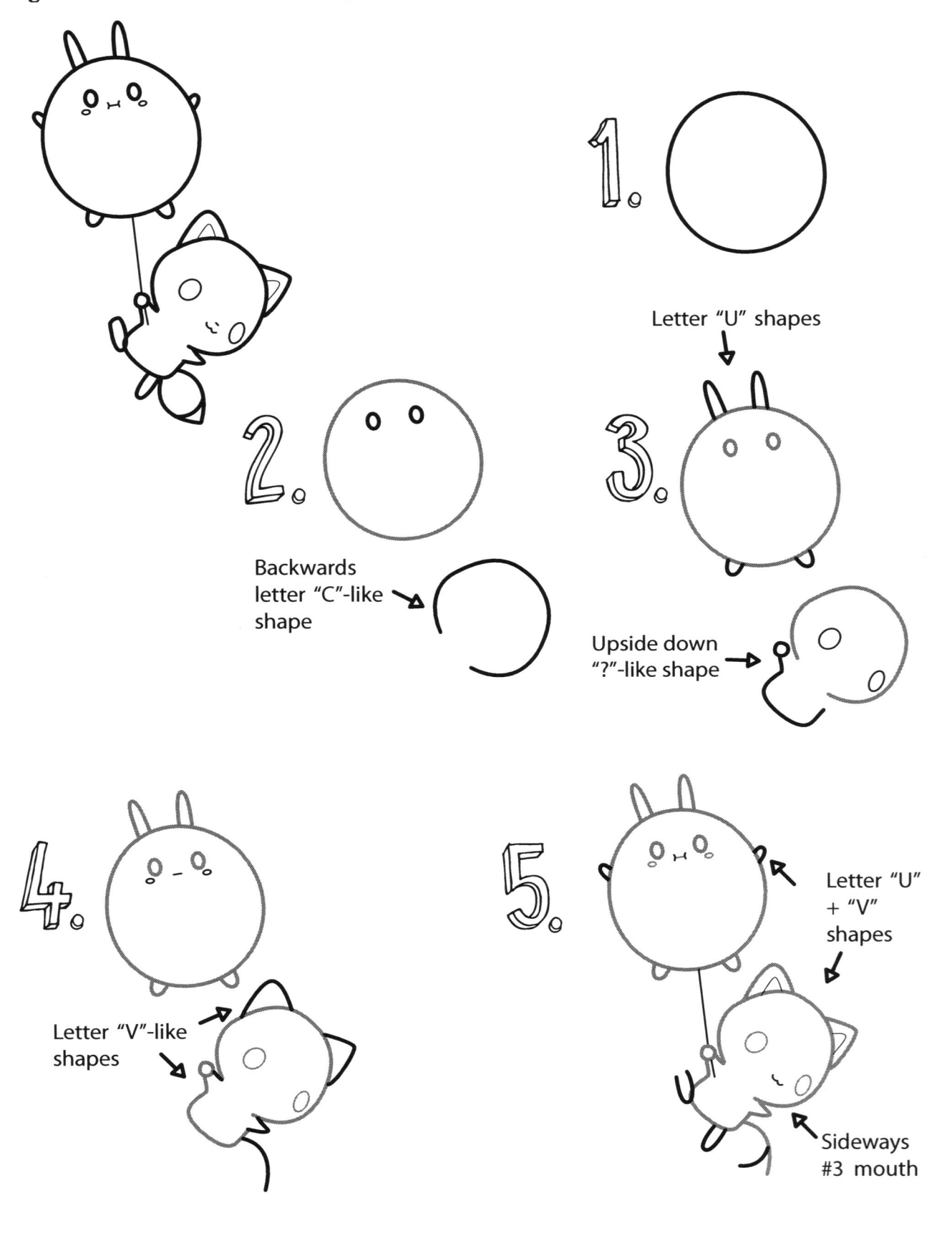

1.

2. Backwards letter "C"-like shape

3. Letter "U" shapes

Upside down "?"-like shape

4. Letter "V"-like shapes

5. Letter "U" + "V" shapes

Sideways #3 mouth

6.

NOW YOU TRY

BEAR IN BUNNY COSTUME

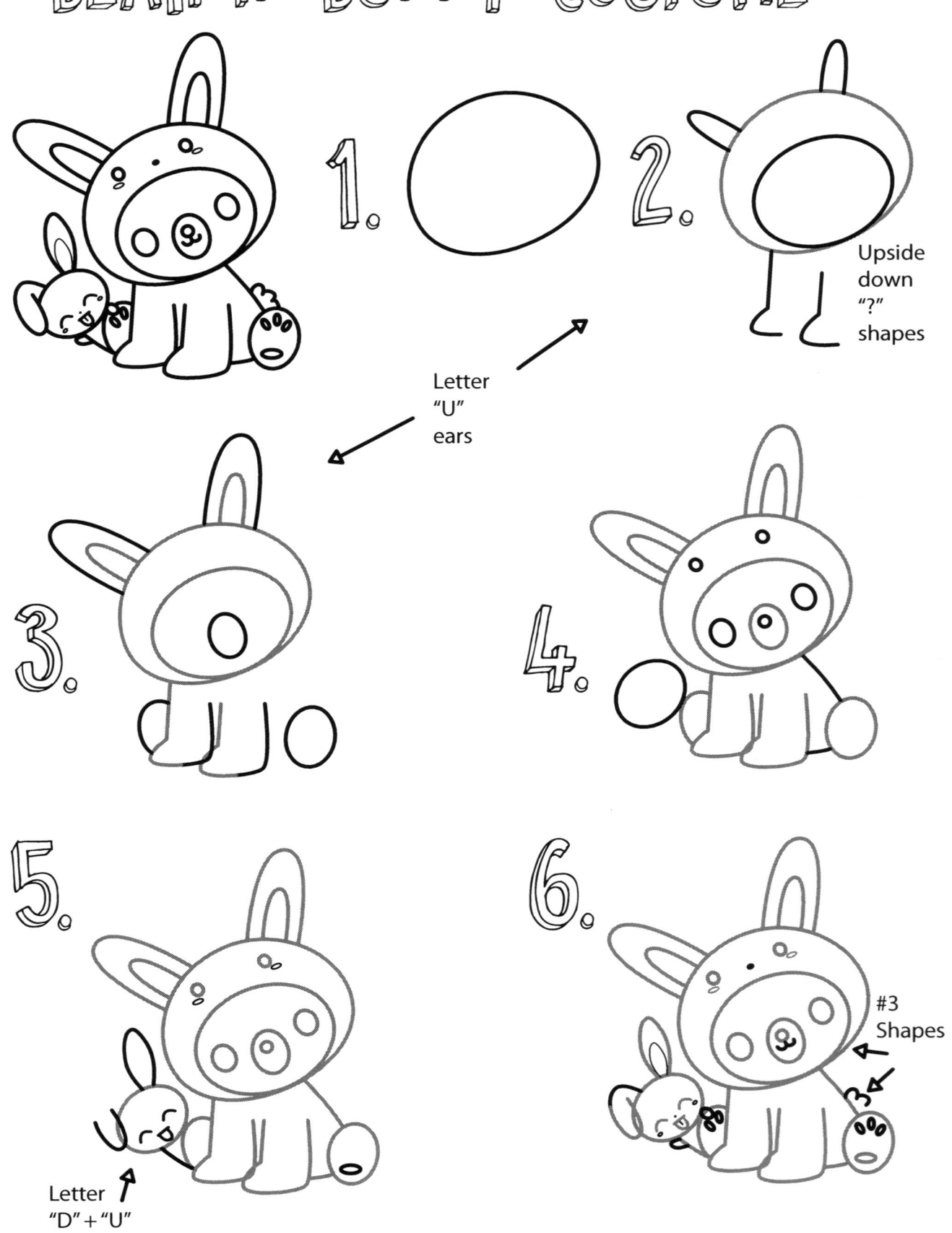

1.

2. Upside down "?" shapes

Letter "U" ears

3.

4.

5. Letter "D" + "U"

6. #3 Shapes

7.

Erase on dotted lines

NOW YOU TRY

HEDGEHOG WITH FLOWER

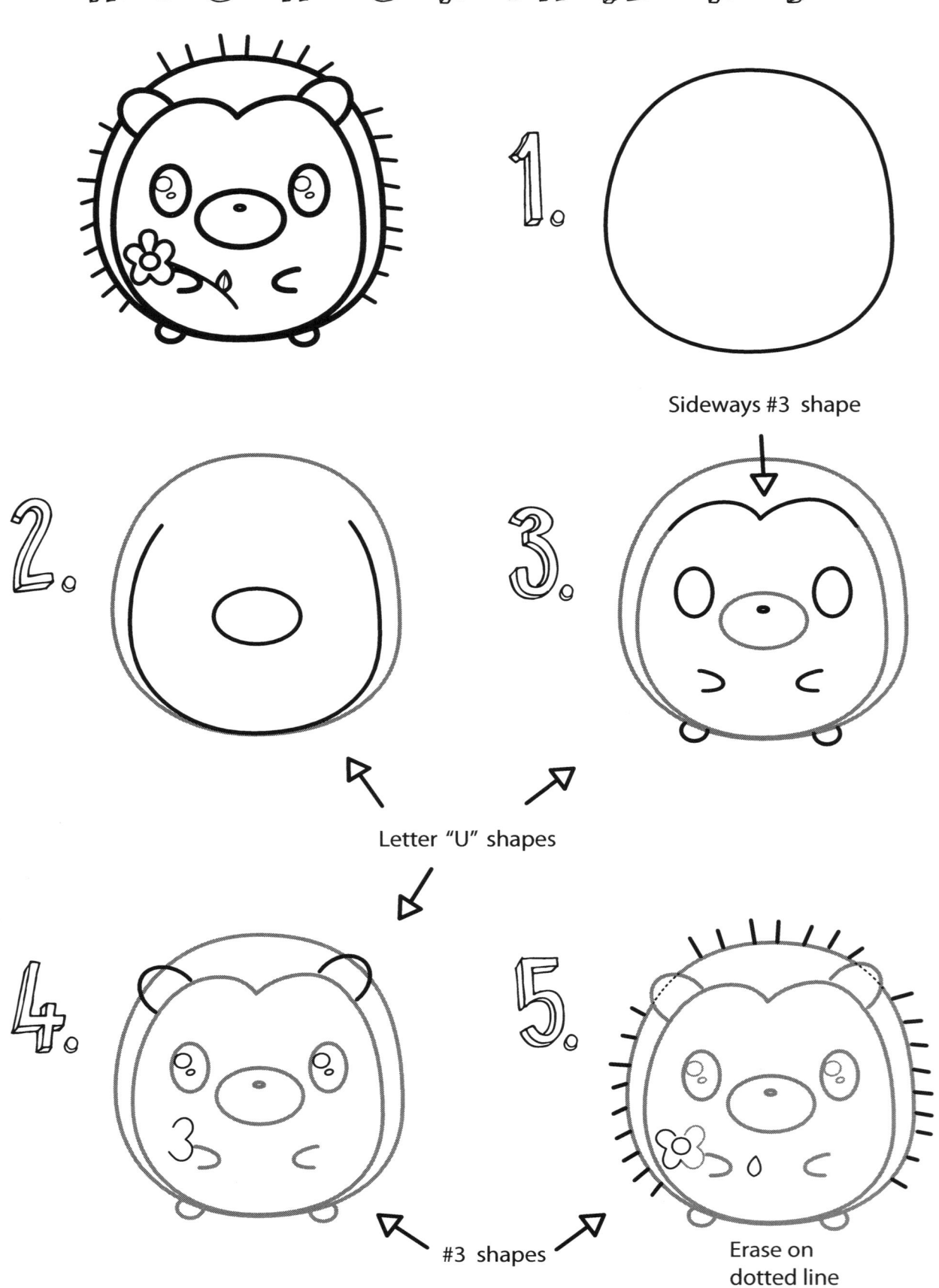

1. Sideways #3 shape

2.

3.

Letter "U" shapes

4.

5. Erase on dotted line

#3 shapes

6.

NOW YOU TRY

BUNNY RIDING RUBBER DUCKY

1. #8 shape

2. Sideways letters "C" + "V"

3. Sideways #3 + "C"

4.

5. Erase on dotted line

6.

Letter "U" ears

NOW YOU TRY

DOGGY LOVES HIS HAMSTER

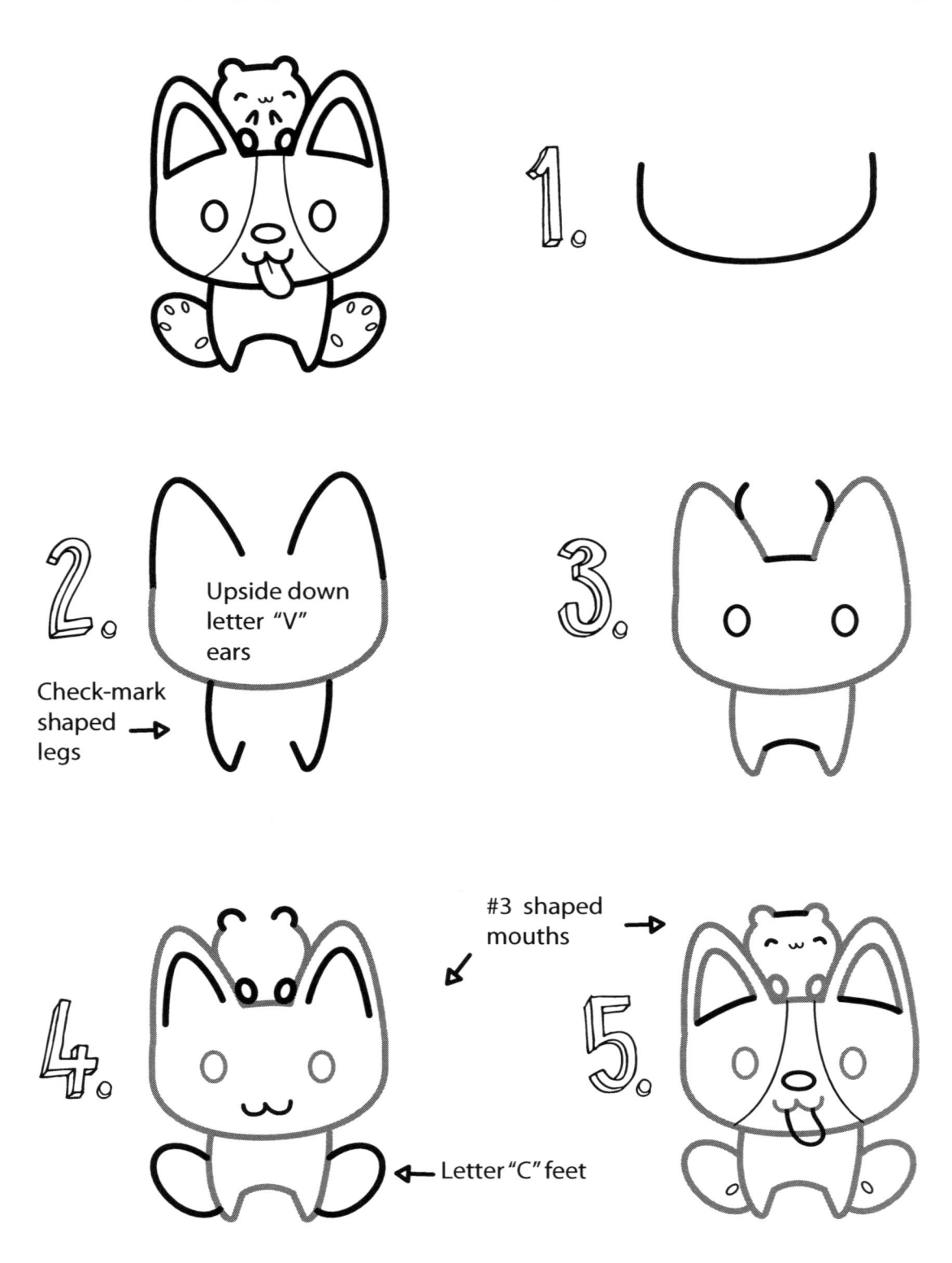

1.

2. Upside down letter "V" ears
   Check-mark shaped legs →

3.

4. #3 shaped mouths →
   ← Letter "C" feet

5.

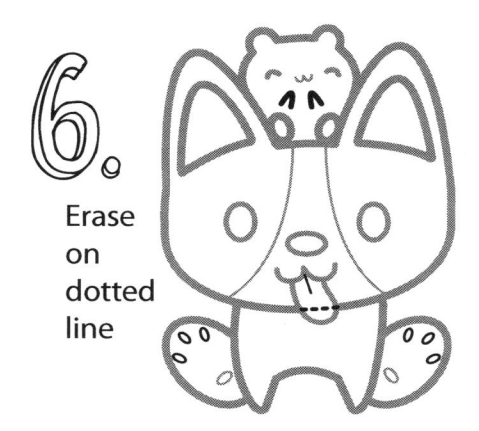

6.
Erase on dotted line

NOW YOU TRY

KID IN FROG COSTUME WITH FROG

1.

2.

#3 shapes

3.

4.

Erase on dotted line

← #5 + "?" shapes

5.

Letter "V" bangs

NOW YOU TRY

RACCOON DREAMING ABOUT PIZZA

1.

2.

3. Letter "V"-like shapes

4. Letter "V"-like shapes

Erase the dotted lines

5.

#3 shape

NOW YOU TRY

OWL AND BAT BUDDIES

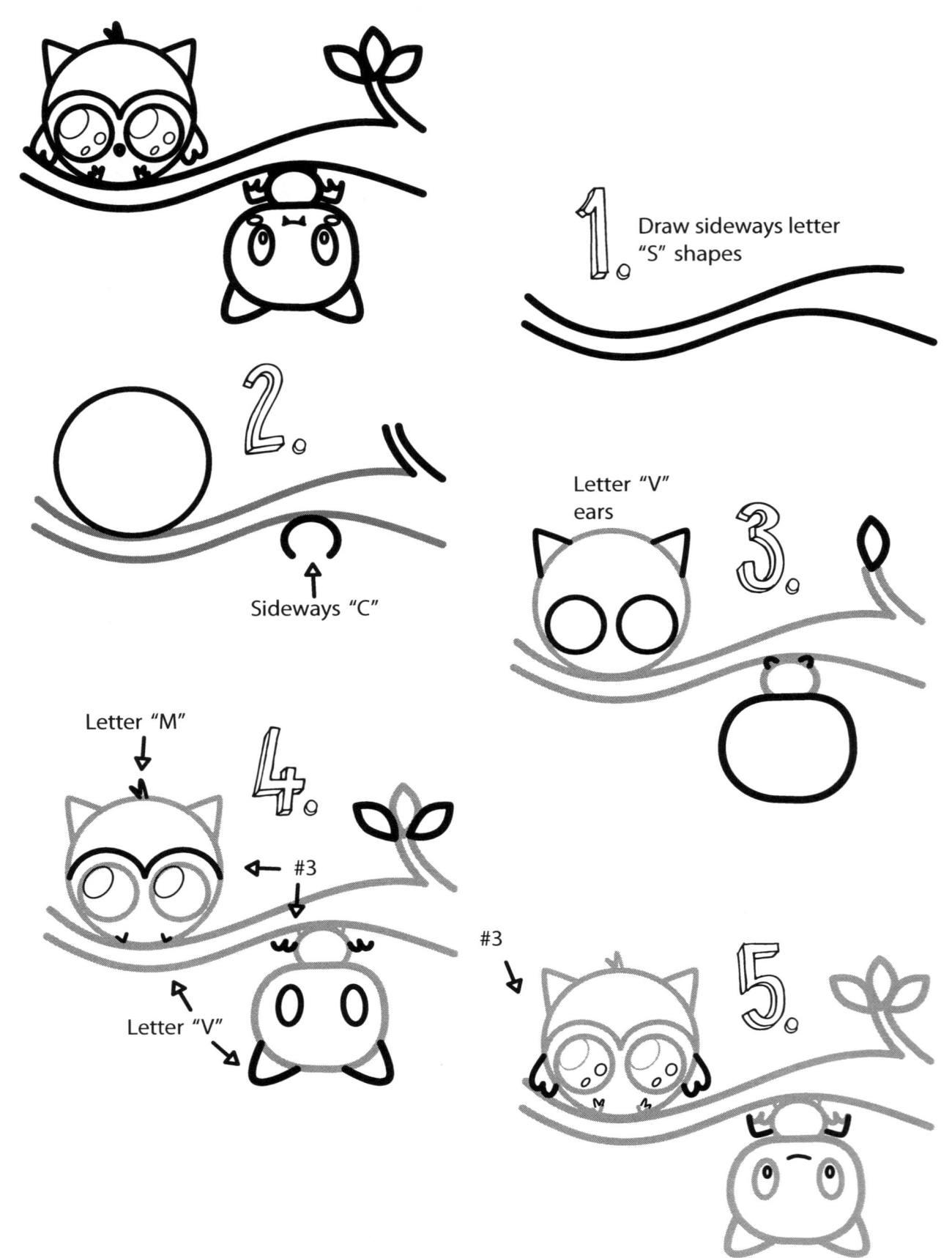

1. Draw sideways letter "S" shapes

2. Sideways "C"

3. Letter "V" ears

4. Letter "M" — #3 — Letter "V"

5. #3

6.

"U" + "V"

NOW YOU TRY

DOGGY BUTT

1.

2. #7-like ears

3. #3-like shapes
Erase on dotted line

4. Letter "J" shapes

5. "?"-like shape

6.

Erase on dotted line

Letter "X" shape

NOW YOU TRY

KITTY LOVES FISHY

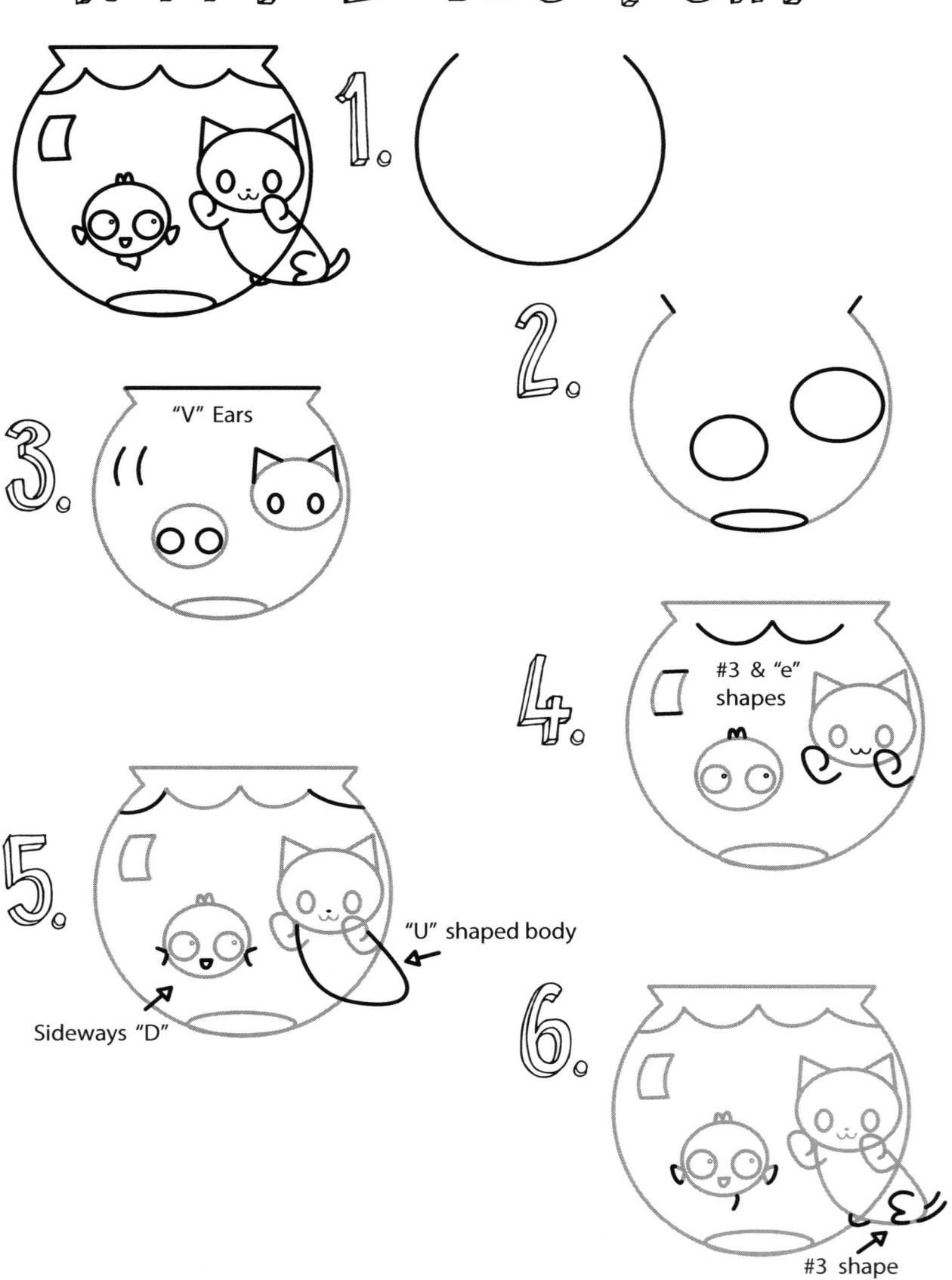

1.

2.

3. "V" Ears

4. #3 & "e" shapes

5. "U" shaped body
   Sideways "D"

6. #3 shape

7.

Erase on dotted lines

Backwards "?"-like shape

NOW YOU TRY

KID IN UNICORN COSTUME EATS GUMMY BEAR

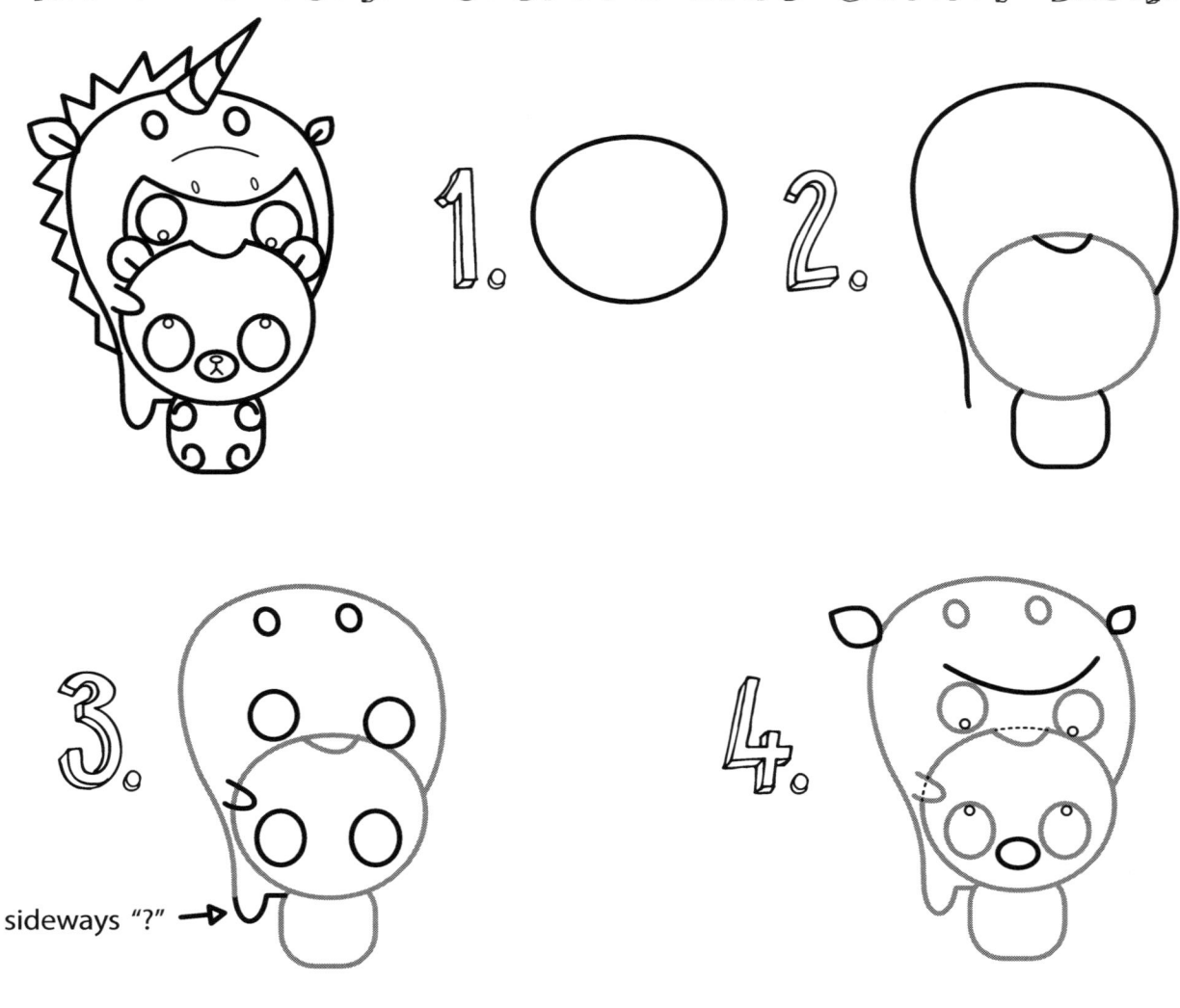

1.

2.

3. sideways "?"

4. Don't draw the dotted lines

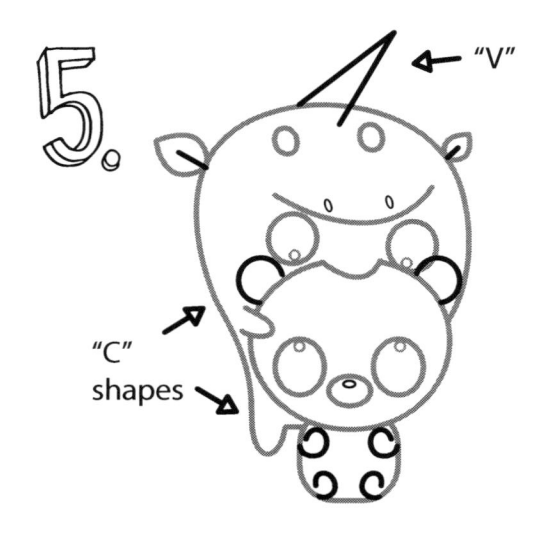

5. "V"
   "C" shapes

6. "Y" mouth

7.

NOW YOU TRY

PIG CUPCAKE

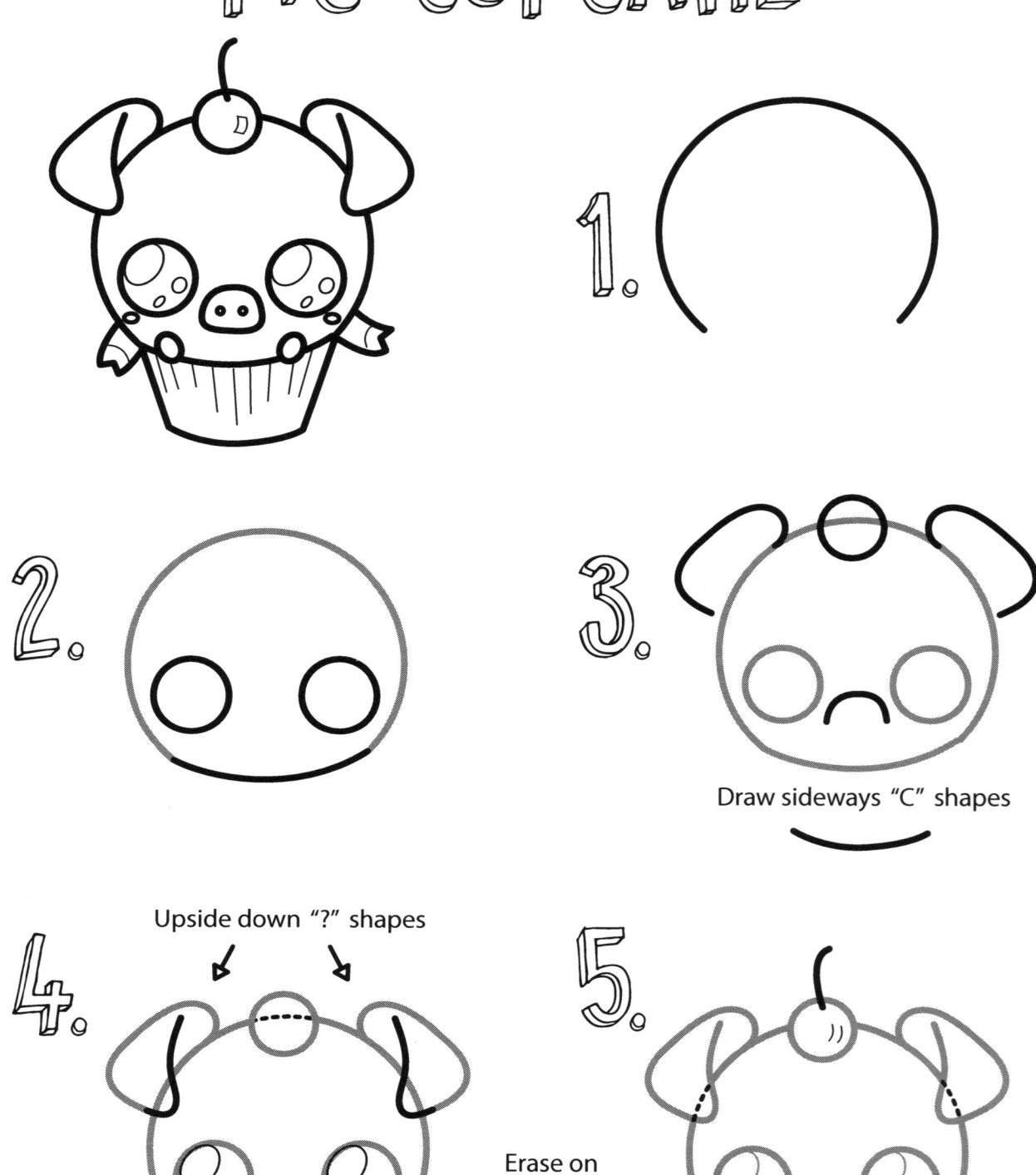

1.

2.

3. Draw sideways "C" shapes

4. Upside down "?" shapes

5. Erase on dotted lines

"M" shapes

6.

NOW YOU TRY

SEAL CONE

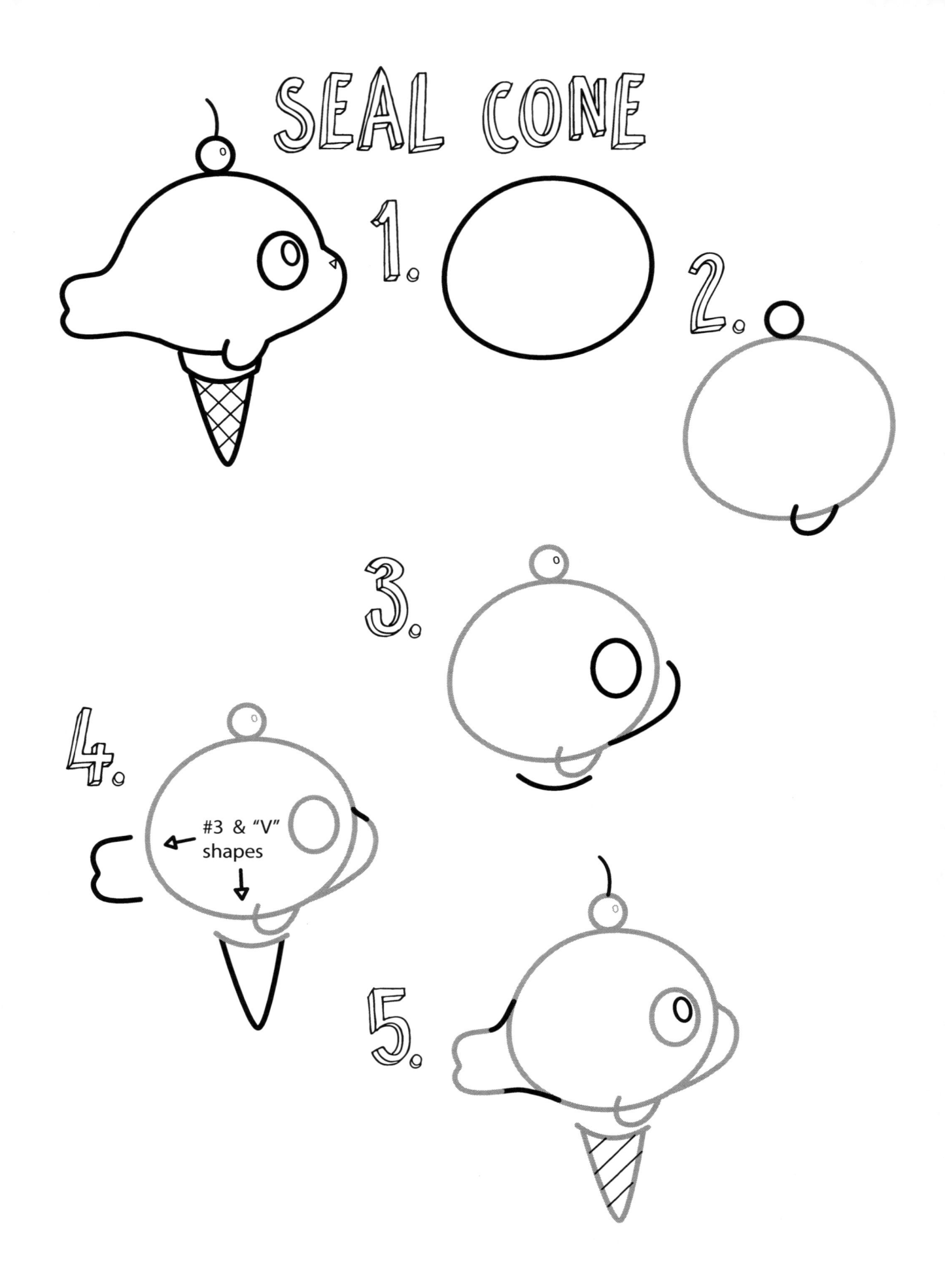

1.
2.
3.
4. #3 & "V" shapes
5.

6.

Erase the dotted lines

NOW YOU TRY

TURTLE DONUT

1.

2.

3.

4. Erase on dotted line

5. Draw wavy line along bottom of the donut

Sideways #3 shapes

6.

NOW YOU TRY

MONSTER BUDDIES

1.

2. Curved "A" shapes

3. "C" shape

   Erase on dotted lines

4. "W" shape

5. #3 shapes

6. "V"-like shapes

7.
Erase on dotted line

NOW YOU TRY

SHARK COSTUME

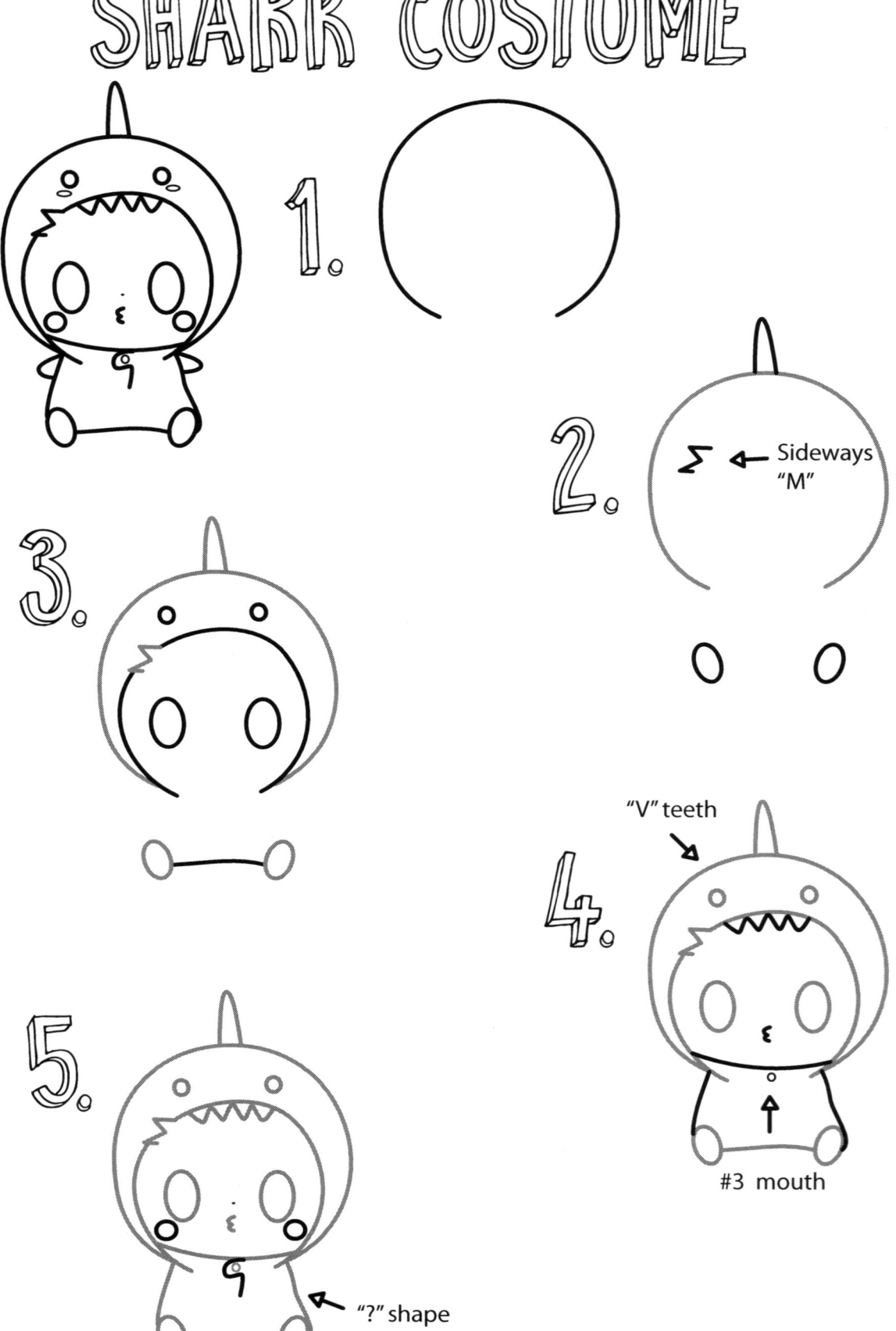

1.

2. Sideways "M"

3.

4. "V" teeth

#3 mouth

5. "?" shape

6.

NOW YOU TRY

CUTESY PLATYPUS

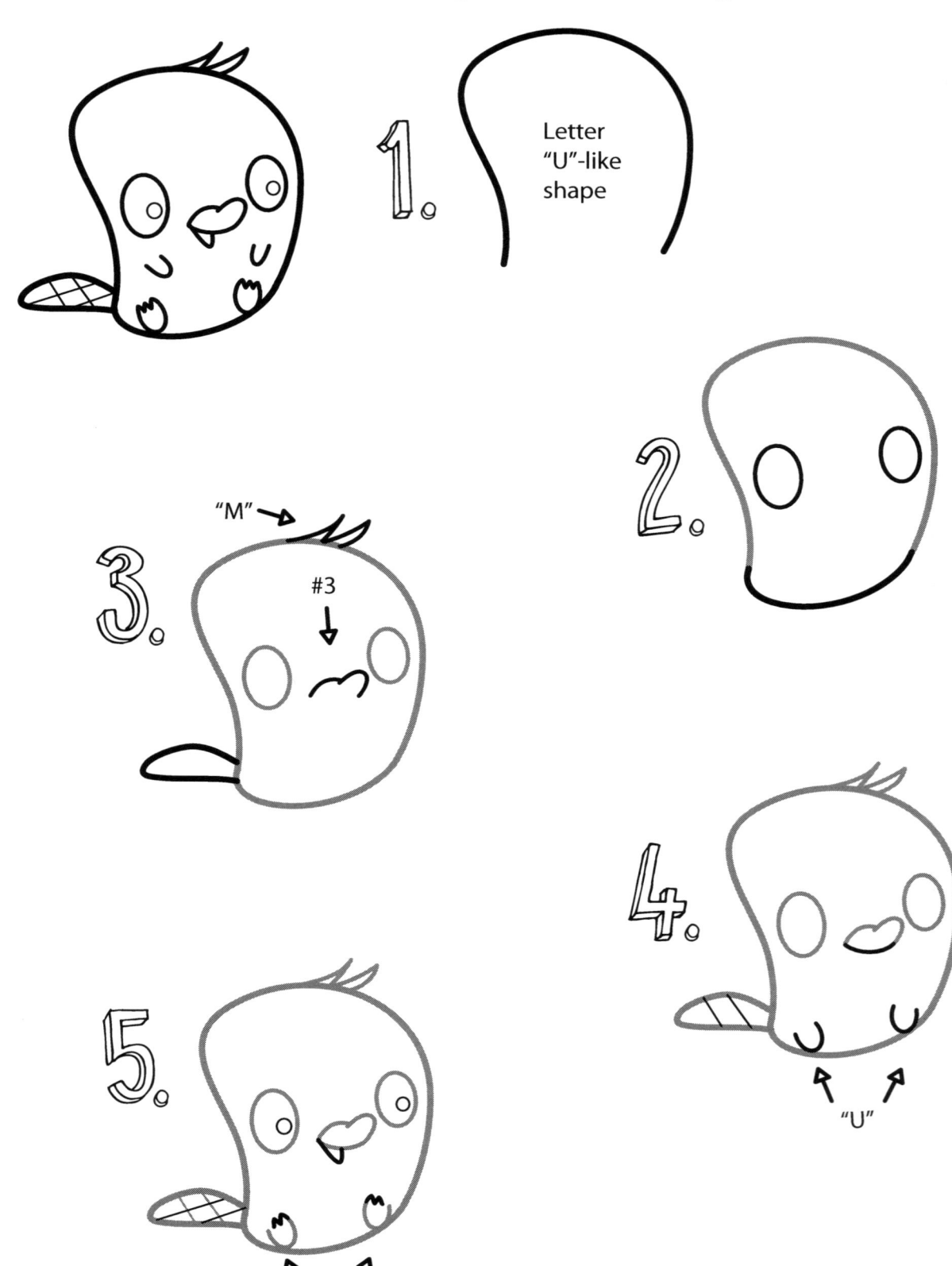

1. Letter "U"-like shape

2.

3. "M" → #3 ↓

4. "U"

5. "M"

6.

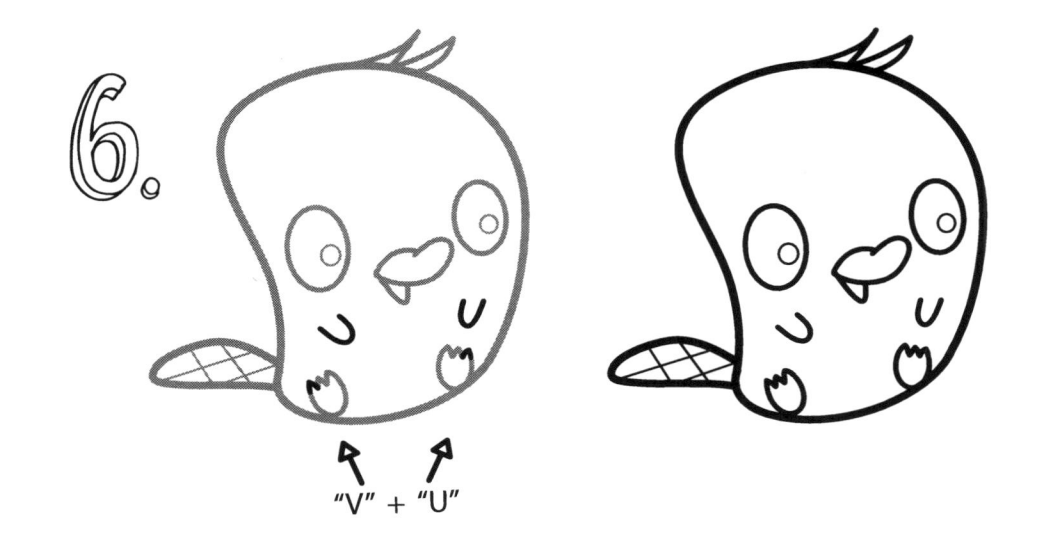

"V" + "U"

NOW YOU TRY

STACKED KITTIES

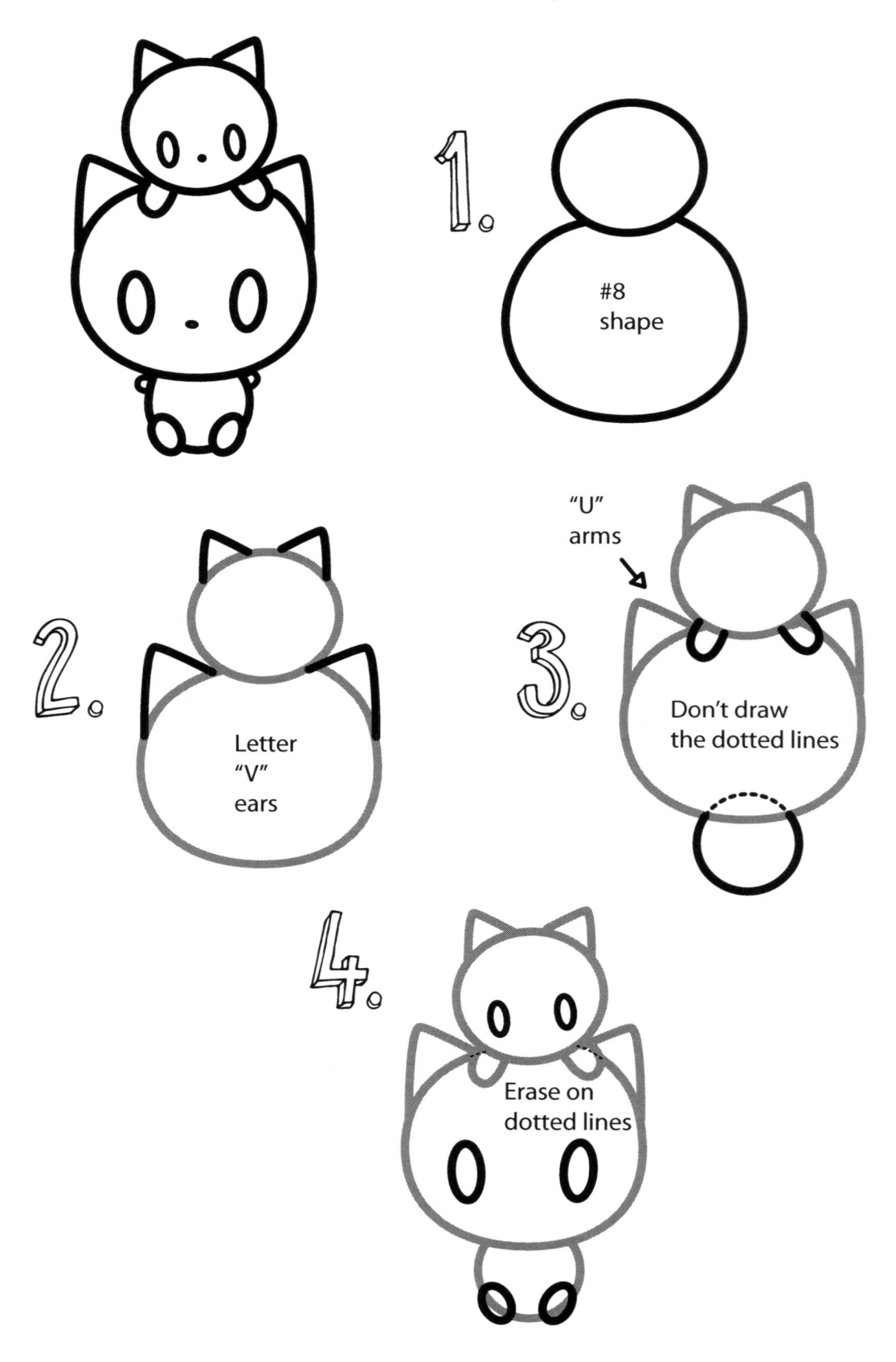

1. #8 shape

2. Letter "V" ears

3. "U" arms — Don't draw the dotted lines

4. Erase on dotted lines

5.

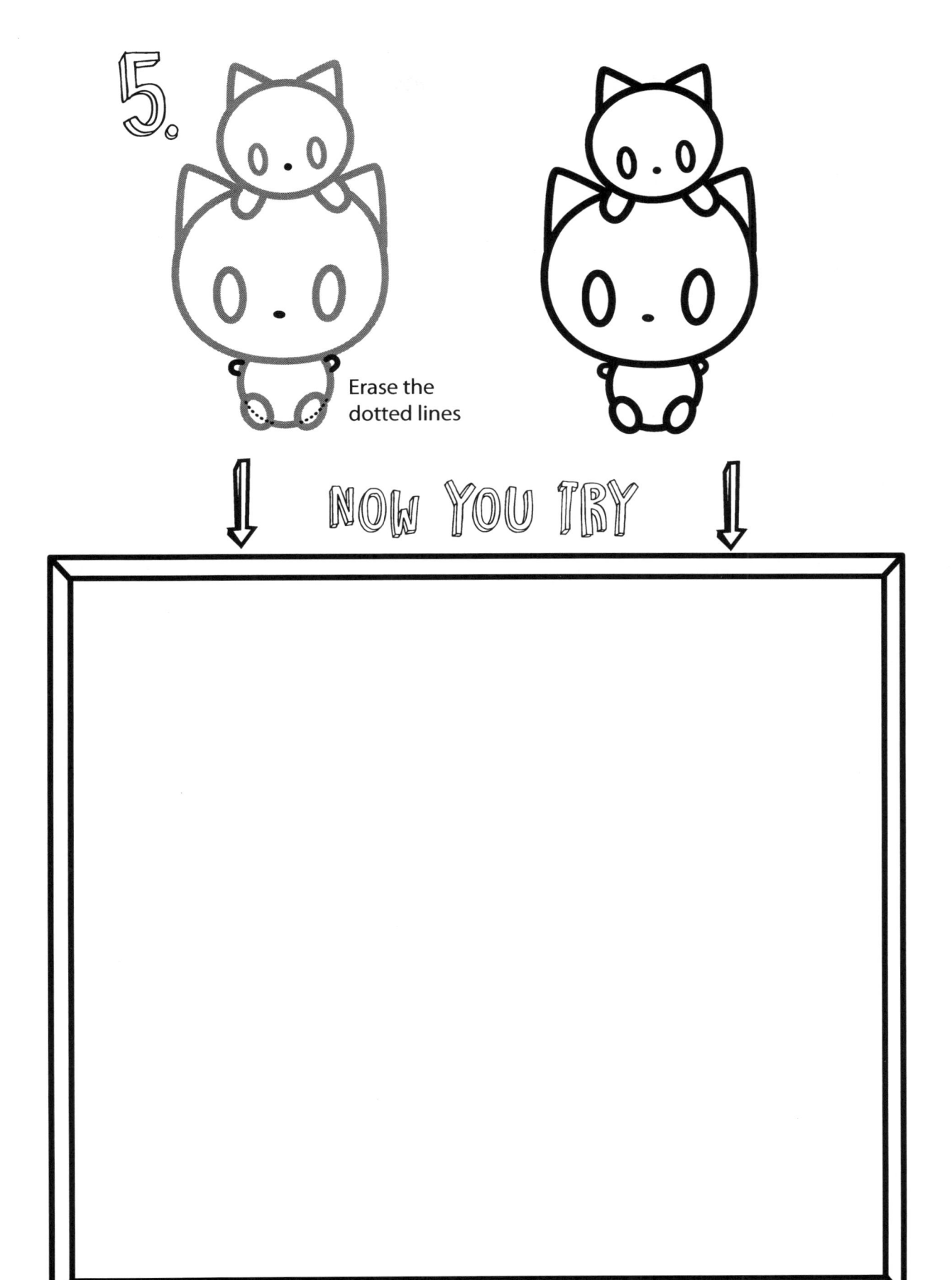

Erase the dotted lines

NOW YOU TRY

FISH SPITTING ON BIRD

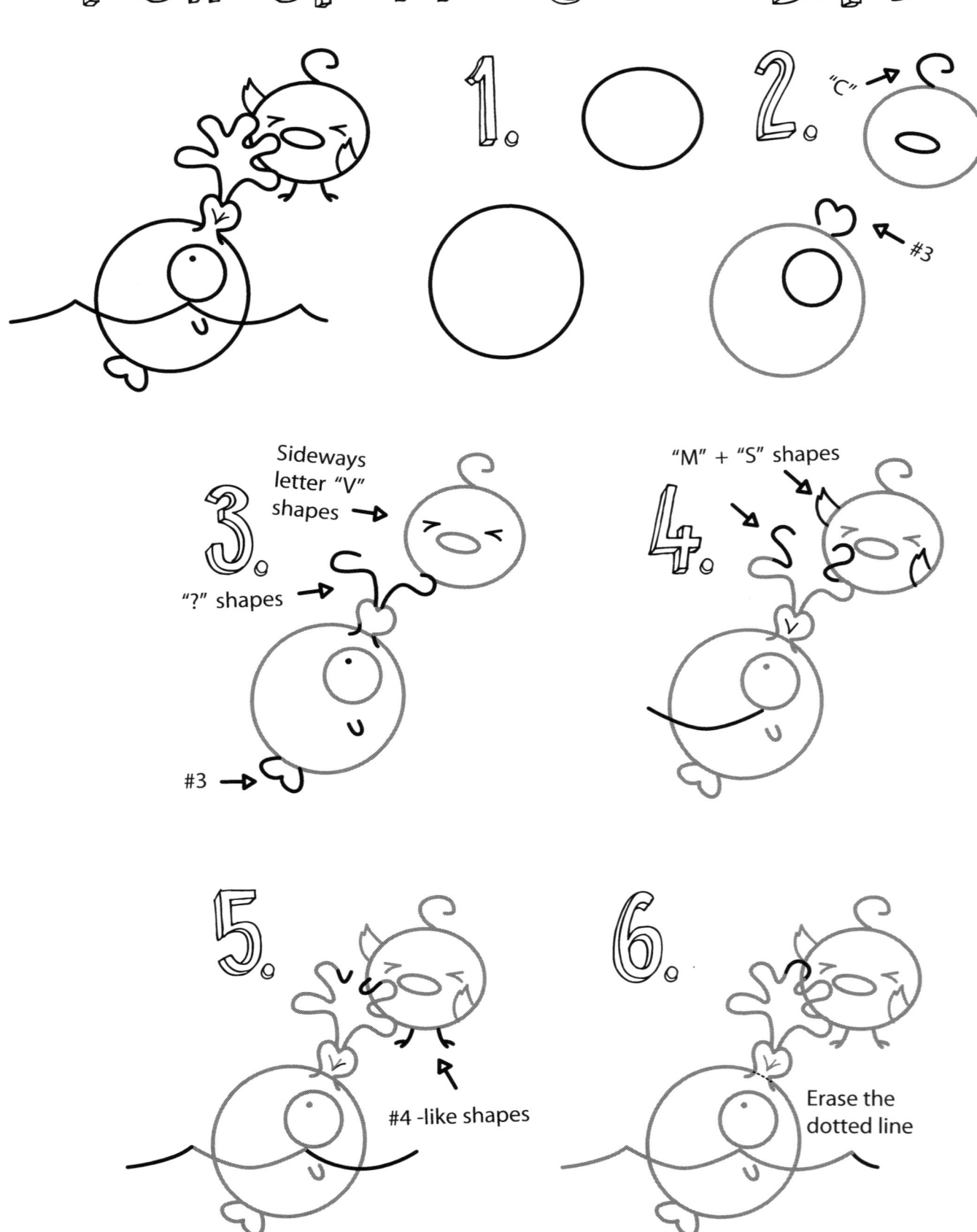

1.

2. "C" →

#3

3. Sideways letter "V" shapes →

"?" shapes →

#3 →

4. "M" + "S" shapes →

5. #4 -like shapes

6. Erase the dotted line

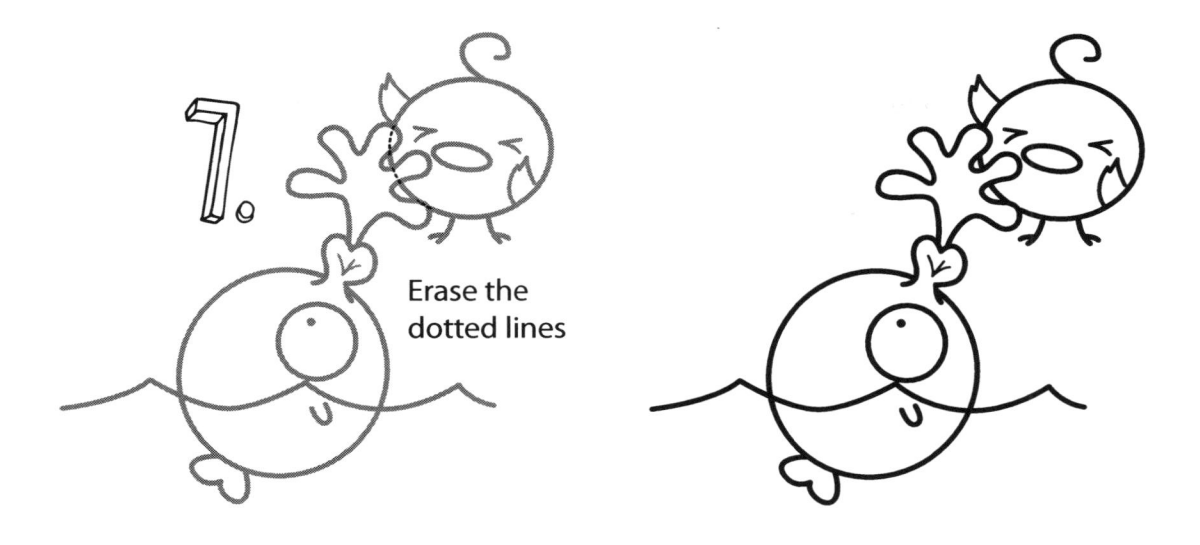

7. Erase the dotted lines

NOW YOU TRY

MOUSE AND HER BALLOON

1. Sideways letter "D"

2.

3.

4.

5. Erase the dotted lines

6.

NOW YOU TRY

CUTESY TIGER

1.

2. Don't draw the dotted lines

3. #3 shapes

Letter "V" shapes

4.

5.

6. Letter "U" arms

7. Erase on dotted line

NOW YOU TRY

SEAL WITH PENGUIN BALL

1.

2.

3. Sideways #3 shape

Erase on dotted lines

4. #3

5.

Erase on dotted line

NOW YOU TRY

TURTLE EATING PIZZA

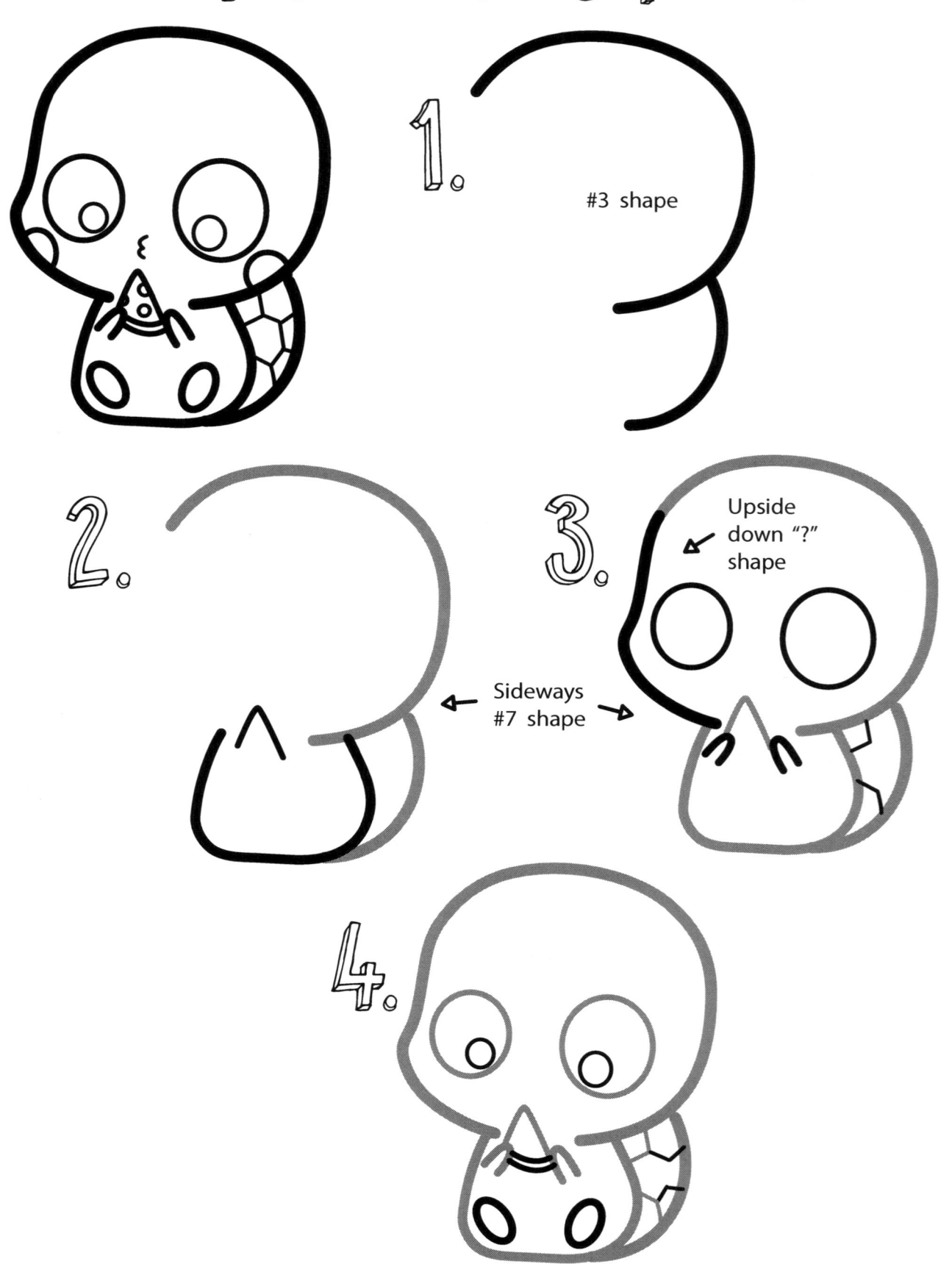

1. #3 shape

2. Sideways #7 shape

3. Upside down "?" shape

4.

#3 shaped mouth

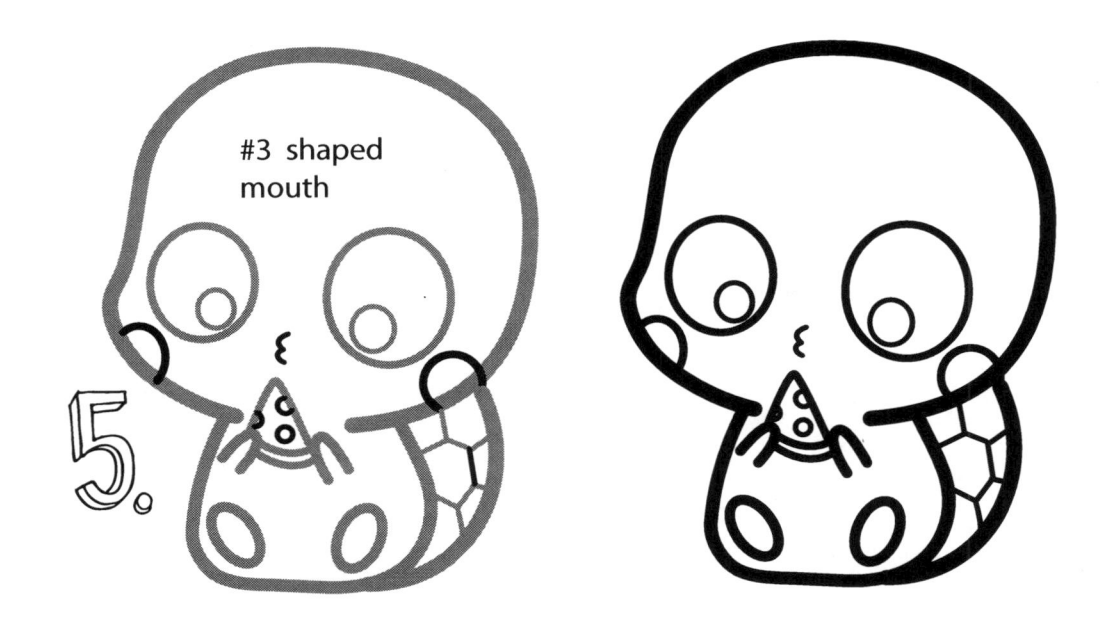

5.

NOW YOU TRY

CUTE ICE CREAM CONE

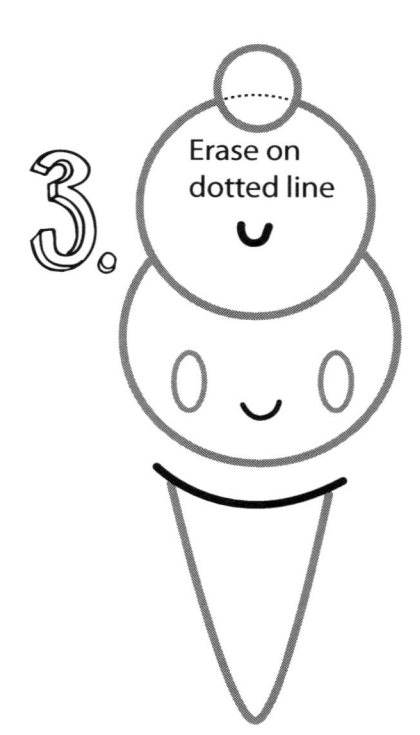

1. #8 shape

   Don't draw the dotted lines

2. "V" shape

3. Erase on dotted line

4. Sideways #3 shapes

5.

NOW YOU TRY

CUTE FRENCH FRIES

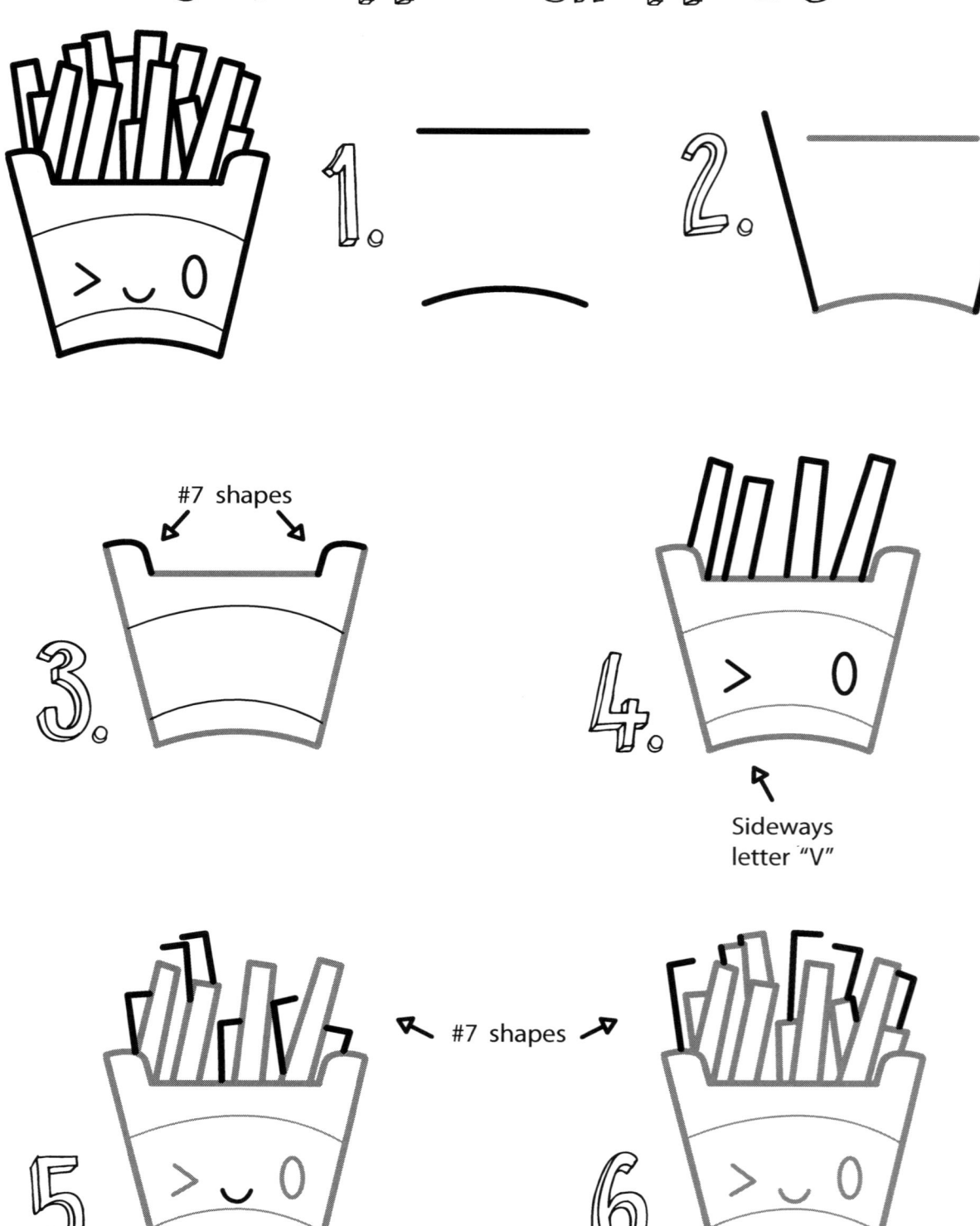

1.

2.

3. #7 shapes

4. Sideways letter "V"

5. #7 shapes

6.

7.

NOW YOU TRY

OUR OTHER BOOKS

Please Give Us Good Reviews on Amazon! This book is self-published so we need to get the word out! **If You Give us a 5 Star Review**, and Email us About it, We Will Do a Tutorial Per Your Child's Request and Post it On DrawingHowToDraw.com

Printed in Poland
by Amazon Fulfillment
Poland Sp. z o.o., Wrocław